Original title:
Growing Together in Friendship

Copyright © 2024 Swan Charm
All rights reserved.

Author: Eliora Lumiste
ISBN HARDBACK: 978-9916-89-061-5
ISBN PAPERBACK: 978-9916-89-062-2
ISBN EBOOK: 978-9916-89-063-9

## **Weaving Threads of Affection**

In the quiet of the night,
We share whispers soft and light.
Every moment that we hold,
Threads of silver, threads of gold.

With laughter woven through our days,
In gentle hearts, love always stays.
Through storms and sun, we find our way,
In this tapestry we lay.

**Together We Flourish**

Two seeds planted side by side,
In harmony, we learn to ride.
With every breeze, we reach up high,
Together, we touch the sky.

In gardens bright, we find our place,
Each bloom a smile, each leaf a grace.
With roots entwined, we stand as one,
Together, we bask in the sun.

## **Embracing the Journey**

Step by step, we find our way,
In every moment, come what may.
With open hearts, we grasp the day,
Together, we will not sway.

Through valleys low and mountains high,
In the embrace, we learn to fly.
With every turn, a brand new sight,
Side by side, hearts full of light.

## Laughter in the Sunshine

Under skies so vast and blue,
We share laughter, pure and true.
In each heartbeat, joy we find,
With sunny smiles, our lives entwined.

As petals dance upon the breeze,
We chase the warmth, find our ease.
With every chuckle, every cheer,
In the sunshine, love draws near.

**Roots of Connection**

In the earth, we find our way,
Tangled roots beneath the clay.
From each whisper, bonds do grow,
In silent strength, we learn to know.

Hands entwined in shared embrace,
In every laugh, a sacred space.
Through storms we stand, unyielding, true,
Together, we rise, anew.

**Blossoms of Bond**

Petals dancing in the breeze,
Each color tells a tale with ease.
In gardens bright, our spirits soar,
With every bloom, we seek for more.

Sunlight filtering through the trees,
Whispers of love carried on the breeze.
In harmony, our hearts do sing,
Together, we embrace the spring.

## Seasons of Trust

Leaves of green turn to gold,
Stories of warmth and trust unfold.
In winter's chill, we find our fire,
Through every season, we inspire.

With every cycle, we grow strong,
In sun and snow, we know we belong.
Roots run deep in earth's embrace,
In every heartbeat, time and space.

## **The Harmony of Hearts**

In melodies that softly play,
Two hearts beat in their own way.
With notes entwined, a song we share,
In every rhythm, love's repair.

The dance of souls in twilight's glow,
In perfect steps, together we flow.
Through silence, laughter, tears, and grace,
In harmony, we find our place.

**Growing Through Seasons**

In spring, we start anew,
With blossoms bright and dew.
Summer brings a blazing sun,
Our laughter and our joy begun.

Autumn paints with golden hues,
As leaves dance down and cruise.
Winter wraps in quiet white,
We gather close and share the light.

# The Roots That Bind

Beneath the soil, we intertwine,
Our stories shared, our strength aligns.
Through storms we sway, but won't break down,
Together we stand, in kinship grown.

Deep in the earth, our past remains,
Each whisper of love, our blood sustains.
In unity, we find our grace,
The roots below, our strong embrace.

## **Community of Hearts**

In every smile, a warm embrace,
We lift each other, find our place.
Together we rise, together we fall,
In this bond, we conquer all.

The laughter shared, the tears we shed,
With every word, our spirits fed.
Hand in hand, we chase the dream,
In harmony, we are a team.

### The Lanterns We Hold


When darkness falls and shadows creep,
We shine our lights, the secrets keep.
With flickering flames, we light the way,
In unity, we won't dismay.

Each lantern bright, a story told,
A path of hope for hearts so bold.
Together we carry the fire's glow,
As dawn breaks through, we rise and grow.

## Seasons of Trust

In springtime's bloom, our hopes arise,
With gentle whispers, beneath clear skies.
The warmth of days, a tender embrace,
In trust we gather, a sacred space.

As summer shines, our laughter flows,
In golden light, affection grows.
With every breeze that softly sings,
We hold together, the joy it brings.

Autumn's hues, a change in time,
We share the burdens, our hearts in rhyme.
With falling leaves, our worries cease,
In trust renewed, we find our peace.

Then winter's chill, a quiet call,
In frosty nights, we stand not small.
With fireside tales, we warm our hands,
In every season, together we stand.

## **Weaving Ties**

In moments shared, our hearts entwine,
With every thread, a love divine.
An tapestry of dreams we cast,
In colors bright, our bond holds fast.

Through laughter's dance, we find our way,
In shadows deep, we choose to stay.
Each secret whispered, a knot we tie,
With strength and grace, we learn to fly.

When storms do brew, we stand as one,
In darkest hours, the light is spun.
With each embrace, we feel the cheer,
In woven ties, there's naught to fear.

With every moment, our lives combine,
In every heartbeat, a sacred sign.
Together we rise, through thick and thin,
In the bonds we cherish, our lives begin.

## **Shared Sunlight**

Under golden skies, we seek the light,
With open hearts, we shine so bright.
In gentle rays, our laughter plays,
Together we dance through sunlit days.

With every dawn, new hopes take flight,
In every shadow, we find our might.
Through fields of dreams, our spirits soar,
In shared sunlight, we yearn for more.

As twilight whispers, the stars will glow,
In quiet moments, our feelings flow.
Together we savor the fading day,
In warmth we trust, come what may.

With every sunset, a promise near,
In dreams we share, there's naught to fear.
Through every season, our joy ignites,
In shared sunlight, our love unites.

## Harvest of Laughter

In fields of joy, we plant the seeds,
With laughter's echo, our heart's true needs.
Through pruning vines and autumn's cheer,
We gather moments, year after year.

With every jest, a bond we grow,
In sunny meadows, where rivers flow.
Together we reap the smiles we've sown,
In laughter's harvest, we've always grown.

As seasons change, our spirits rise,
With every giggle, the heart complies.
The fruits of love, so sweet and bright,
In laughter's glow, we find our light.

In gatherings warm, our stories spin,
With memories sweet, we feel the win.
For in this harvest, we find our way,
With laughter's bounty, we greet each day.

## Blossoms of Bond

In the spring we find our way,
Through petals soft, we dance and play.
A fragrance sweet, a gentle breeze,
Together, bound by love's decrees.

Each bloom a memory we share,
Sun-kissed moments, stripped of care.
A garden rich with colors bright,
In every shade, our hearts take flight.

With roots entwined, we stand so tall,
Through storms and sun, we rise, we fall.
In nature's arms, we find our ground,
In every whisper, love is found.

## The Garden of Us

In the garden where we grow,
Nature's touch, a gentle flow.
With every leaf, our story blooms,
A tapestry of shared perfumes.

Together we sow seeds of trust,
In every moment, love is just.
With sun and rain, our bond will thrive,
In this haven, we are alive.

Through seasons change, we find our way,
In vibrant hues, we laugh and play.
The fruit of care, in hearts it stays,
In this garden, love always stays.

## **Threads of Connection**

A fragile thread, yet strong and true,
Woven tight in skies of blue.
Across the miles, our hearts will sew,
A tapestry of love's warm glow.

Each stitch a memory, rich and bright,
In every laughter, in every flight.
With hands held high, we thread the seam,
In dreams we rise; in hopes, we gleam.

Through time and space, we stand as one,
In shadows cast, we chase the sun.
With every knot, our spirits blend,
In this dance, there is no end.

## Hand in Hand

Hand in hand, we walk this way,
With hopes and dreams for yesterday.
Each step we take, a promise made,
In the glow of twilight's fade.

With fingers clasped, our fears subside,
In silent strength, love is our guide.
Through paths unknown, we wander free,
In every heartbeat, you and me.

With laughter bright, we chase the storms,
In joy and pain, our love transforms.
Side by side, we face the night,
With courage found, our hearts take flight.

## Heart to Heart

In whispers soft, our hearts confide,
In dreams we share, no need to hide.
Connected deep, with souls aligned,
In every beat, true love we find.

Through trials faced, we stand so strong,
In every note, our love's sweet song.
With every tear, the close we stay,
In whispered vows, we find our way.

With open hearts, we seek the light,
Hand in heart, we'll soar in flight.
Together bound, we share this part,
In every moment, heart to heart.

## Together in the Meadow

Beneath the sky so wide and blue,
We wander through the flowers' hue.
With laughter echoing in the breeze,
Together we find moments to seize.

The sun embraces every step we take,
As nature sings, our hearts awake.
With every footfall, whispers of peace,
In this meadow, our worries cease.

The colors dance, a vibrant show,
In this garden where love can grow.
Hand in hand, we share our dreams,
In the stillness, it softly gleams.

The evening glows with a golden light,
Beneath the stars, our souls take flight.
Together we'll chase the fireflies,
In this dance, where joy never dies.

# The Ties that Bind

In every heart, a thread is spun,
An unseen bond, where love's begun.
Through trials faced and laughter shared,
It's in these ties, our spirits paired.

Moments fleeting, yet deeply sown,
In friendship's soil, we have grown.
Like roots entwined beneath the ground,
In unity, our strength is found.

Through storms that test, and times of strife,
We hold each other, giving life.
With every tear, a lesson learned,
These ties of love, forever burned.

So let us cherish every day,
In this tapestry, come what may.
Together we'll weave our story's thread,
In every word that's left unsaid.

## Reflections in the Stream

With every ripple, stories flow,
Carried gently, soft and slow.
Beneath the surface, worlds reside,
In tranquil waters, secrets hide.

The trees lean down to catch a glance,
In mirrored depths, they find a chance.
To witness blooms in nature's art,
Reflecting life, a sacred heart.

As pebbles stir, disturbance fades,
The stream reveals the light it shades.
In silence, whispers of the past,
Each moment treasured, fleeting, vast.

When dusk descends with shades of gold,
The waters speak of tales untold.
A simple glance, a fleeting gleam,
In the flowing wave, we find our dream.

## A Circle of Smiles

In a circle wide, we gather near,
With warm embraces, spreading cheer.
Each smile shared, a gentle glow,
In this moment, love will flow.

The laughter dances in the air,
As hearts connect, a bond we share.
With stories spun and joys expressed,
Together, we are truly blessed.

Through peaks and valleys, hand in hand,
We weave our dreams, a vibrant band.
With every hug, a promise made,
In this circle, fears will fade.

The light within each face we see,
Reflects the joy of you and me.
A tapestry of hope and grace,
In every smile, we find our place.

## **Waves of Friendship**

In the silence, whispers flow,
Glimmers of trust, seeds we sow.
Together we dance on the tide,
With every wave, we take a ride.

Connection deepens, bonds are made,
In laughter's echo, fears will fade.
From distant shores, hearts entwined,
In this ocean, love defined.

Through storms we weather, side by side,
In every heart, love won't divide.
A lighthouse shines through darkened nights,
Guiding souls to newfound heights.

Every wave, a story told,
Memories cherished, never old.
Together we rise, together we fall,
In waves of friendship, we have it all.

## The Tree of Companionship

In a garden, we planted a tree,
Roots intertwining, you and me.
Branches stretch wide, reaching high,
In the warmth of the sun, we sigh.

Leaves rustle softly, stories share,
In its shade, we find our care.
Seasons change, yet we remain,
Through every joy, through every pain.

Around the trunk, laughter rings,
The strength of friendship, hope it brings.
As we nurture, the tree will grow,
In its embrace, our love will show.

With every bloom, a new delight,
Together we shine, our future bright.
In the tree of companionship we find,
A bond that ties both heart and mind.

## Embracing Difference

Colors and voices, unique and bright,
In our mosaic, we find the light.
Every difference, a note in the song,
Together in harmony, where we belong.

With open hearts, we gather near,
Celebrating all we hold dear.
Diverse as the stars, yet one in the sky,
In embracing difference, we learn to fly.

Hand in hand, we break down walls,
In our acceptance, the spirit calls.
United we stand, together so strong,
In this journey, we all belong.

Through every story, we find our place,
In the beauty of balance, we find grace.
Embracing difference, we grow and thrive,
In this vibrant world, we feel alive.

**Our Shared Journey**

Steps we take on this winding road,
With every mile, our story's owed.
Hand in hand, through thick and thin,
In every challenge, together we win.

With laughter and tears, we tread the path,
Finding joy in every aftermath.
Moments cherished, memories forged,
Side by side, our spirits charged.

Our hearts as one, we face the unknown,
In the depths of love, we've grown.
With every sunset, a new dawn near,
In our shared journey, there's nothing to fear.

Through valleys low and mountains high,
With hope as our guide, we touch the sky.
Together we write this tale so grand,
In our shared journey, forever we'll stand.

## Hopes on the Horizon

Beneath the sky so wide and blue,
Dreams take flight, they break right through.
With every dawn, a chance to rise,
Bright like the sun, igniting the skies.

Whispers of hope dance in the breeze,
Carried gently through the trees.
Tomorrow's promise glimmers near,
A pinprick star that draws us clear.

Mountains stand, stoic and grand,
Yet we climb, we make our stand.
With courage sewn into our seams,
We chase the light, we chase our dreams.

In every heart, a flickering flame,
A silent wish, a loud acclaim.
Together we forge, with every stride,
In unity, our hopes collide.

As twilight falls, we gather round,
In shared silence, peace is found.
With eyes towards the vast expanse,
The horizon calls, we take our chance.

# The Watering Can of Care

In hands so gentle, a can is held,
Sprinkling love where hearts have dwelled.
Each drop a promise, tender and sweet,
Nurturing dreams, making them meet.

With every pour, the soil wakes,
Awakening life, as the heart breaks.
A simple gesture, a small act done,
In the garden of souls, we are one.

Flowers bloom, colors so bright,
Each petal a story, a beacon of light.
Through stormy days and sunny skies,
We water hope, watch it arise.

Roots intertwine, in strength they grow,
A network of trust, deep below.
In every droplet, a vision shared,
In the watering can, we've always cared.

Together we stand, hand in hand,
In the lush garden, we make our stand.
With care as our guide, we'll travel far,
In every heart, there blooms a star.

## **Roots Intertwined**

Beneath the surface, where shadows dwell,
Roots intertwine, they weave their spell.
In silent strength, they find their way,
Connecting lives in the light of day.

Through shared whispers, histories flow,
In every twist, love starts to grow.
We are the trees, and our roots run deep,
In the soil of trust, our secrets keep.

With storms we weather, together we stand,
In moments of trial, a steady hand.
Each challenge faced, each tear we cry,
Thirty years down, and we still fly.

Branches reaching to the vast unknown,
In unity, we've truly grown.
Through storms and sun, our spirits soar,
Together entwined, forever more.

In every heart, an echoing call,
Roots intertwined, we'll never fall.
As seasons change, we find our way,
In the dance of life, we'll always stay.

## A Garden of Hearts

In the garden where love blooms,
Whispers dance on gentle brooms.
Petals soft with hues so bright,
Tender feelings wrapped in light.

Every flower tells a tale,
Of passion's winds that softly sail.
Roots entwined beneath the ground,
In this haven, peace is found.

Sunrise paints the sky in gold,
As secrets of the heart unfold.
Radiant colors blend and weave,
In this space, we laugh, we grieve.

Morning dew like teardrops cling,
To petals where our hopes take wing.
Each bloom a memory, so dear,
In this garden, love draws near.

Evening falls, the stars emerge,
With every sigh, our hearts converge.
In shadows soft, we embrace tight,
In the garden, love ignites.

**Touching Souls**

A glance that speaks without a word,
In silence, hearts can be stirred.
Two souls dance in hidden beats,
In the night, their warmth repeats.

Fingers brush like autumn leaves,
In moments sweet, the heart believes.
A smile shared across the room,
Ignites a spark, dispels the gloom.

In every laugh, a story lives,
A bond that time alone forgives.
Through heavy storms and skies of gray,
Together, they find their way.

Echoes linger from the past,
As memories build, they fade fast.
Yet in the depths, the love remains,
A guiding light through all the pains.

Hands entwined, they walk the line,
Underneath the stars, they shine.
In every touch, a sacred vow,
Forever love, here and now.

**In Synchrony**

Two hearts beating, one strong drum,
Pulsing forth, a love so numb.
In rhythm's grace, they find their song,
Together in a world so strong.

Moments shared, like notes in tune,
Underneath the silver moon.
In every sigh, a gentle flow,
A melody that weaves and grows.

Time stands still when eyes align,
In their gaze, the stars entwine.
With each heartbeat, life unfolds,
A symphony of dreams retold.

Whispers travel on the breeze,
Carried softly through the trees.
Every heartbeat sings a note,
In every dream, their love can float.

In synchrony, they move as one,
Two lives woven, never done.
Together facing all life brings,
In their dance, the universe sings.

## Waves of Affection

Like waves that kiss the golden shore,
Love crashes in, forevermore.
Each tide a whisper, soft and sweet,
In the rhythm, their hearts meet.

Moonlit nights guide their way,
As stars above begin to play.
Underneath the vast expanse,
Two souls entwined in a timeless dance.

With every ebb, they come alive,
In this ocean, they both thrive.
Ripples spread from each embrace,
In the depths, they find their place.

High and low, their spirits rise,
In the currents, love defies.
Navigating through the storms,
In each other, warmth transforms.

As dawn arrives and colors bloom,
Together, they sweep away the gloom.
With waves of affection rolling near,
In their hearts, the world feels clear.

## In Each Other's Shade

Beneath the tree, where whispers sigh,
We find a place where time goes by.
In dappled light, our laughter plays,
Together here, in each other's shade.

The world outside may rush and chase,
Yet in this haven, we find our space.
With every glance, a silent vow,
In this embrace, we live the now.

A gentle breeze, the leaves do sway,
Our hearts entwined, come what may.
In shadows cast, our dreams take flight,
In every glance, a spark of light.

The moments shared, the stories spun,
Two souls as one, our journey's begun.
In laughter bright or tears that fall,
Together still, we have it all.

And as the sun begins to set,
We treasure all, we won't forget.
In every shadow, love is laid,
Forever here, in each other's shade.

**Unfolding Petals**

In the garden where silence grows,
A fragrance sweet, the soft wind blows.
Petals whisper, secrets untold,
In colors bright, their beauty bold.

With each sunrise, they greet the day,
Unfolding slowly, come what may.
A dance of hues, in sunlight's kiss,
A fleeting moment, pure and bliss.

Nature's hands shape every form,
Against the storm, they brave and warm.
In layers deep, their lives unwind,
A testament of love aligned.

Around them buzz, the bees that sing,
In harmony, their joy takes wing.
Together they shine, a colorful array,
In a world that spins, they find their way.

So let us learn from petals' grace,
To bloom and thrive in every place.
In our own time, let hearts connect,
With love unfurling, we will reflect.

## Hearts Alight

In the quiet glow of twilight's spark,
Two hearts beat strong against the dark.
With every glance, a flame ignites,
Together we stand, our spirits light.

The shadows dance, they flicker and sway,
In the warmth of love, we find our way.
Through whispered words and gentle touch,
In this moment, I feel so much.

A symphony of dreams takes flight,
Guided by stars, our hopes are bright.
In every heartbeat, a story told,
Of love entwined, a bond so bold.

As time moves on, we'll face the night,
With hands held tight, our future's bright.
Together we'll chase the dawn's embrace,
In this dance of life, we find our place.

So let us shine, hearts blazing true,
With every breath, I choose you.
In a world so vast, we'll stand our ground,
In love's sweet warmth, forever found.

## The Mosaic of Us

In the tapestry of days gone by,
Each moment woven, a sweet goodbye.
The colors blend, a vibrant hue,
In the mosaic of me and you.

Fragments scattered, yet held so tight,
Together we craft our own delight.
With every tear and every laugh,
We shape the art, we find our path.

In the gentle touch of hands entwined,
A masterpiece of hearts defined.
With every challenge, we find our way,
Creating beauty from the fray.

In shared secrets, our truths emerge,
A quilt of stories, in love we surge.
Each piece unique, yet perfectly placed,
In this grand design, we're interlaced.

So let us cherish our painted past,
In this mosaic, our love will last.
As time unfolds, we'll boldly trust,
In the beauty crafted, the mosaic of us.

## United in Bloom

In gardens where colors entwine,
Petals whisper stories divine.
Hearts open wide, embrace the sun,
Together we flourish, two become one.

Among the willow, laughter sings,
Hope takes root on gentle wings.
With every shadow that we face,
Love's bright light finds its place.

Breezes carry dreams so sweet,
Every heartbeat, a rhythmic beat.
In this union, we grow strong,
With every moment, we belong.

The world may change, yet we remain,
Bound by joy and kissed by rain.
Through seasons' turn, we hold tight,
Hand in hand, in pure delight.

As blossoms dance in evening's glow,
Together we face what life bestows.
In this garden, forever stay,
United in bloom, come what may.

## **Paths Aligned**

Your gaze meets mine, a spark ignites,
Two journeys merging, hearts take flight.
With every step, a tighter weave,
Together we dream, together believe.

Through city streets and moonlit paths,
We chase the dawn, the sound of laughs.
With hands entwined, we navigate,
Craving wonders, never late.

In moments shared, our spirits soar,
Finding treasures we can adore.
Every twist, every turn we trace,
Leads us closer to our safe place.

With shared horizons and starlit skies,
We craft our story, no goodbyes.
Mapping worlds in endless grace,
Together we make our own space.

In the heart of the storm, we find our calm,
In your laughter, I find my balm.
Paths aligned, through thick and thin,
Together forever, we will win.

## The Symphony of Us

In a world of notes, our hearts compose,
Melodies rise as love overflows.
Together we dance to life's sweet tune,
With every heartbeat, our spirits attune.

In whispers soft, our dreams take flight,
Creating harmony in day and night.
As seasons change, our rhythm stays,
Guiding each other through winding ways.

With every laugh, a sweet refrain,
Healing echoes, love's sweet gain.
Through tempests fierce, we hold the ground,
In the silence, our hearts resound.

The symphony swells, bright and bold,
Each note a memory, a story told.
Together we weave life's masterpiece,
In laughter and tears, we find our peace.

So let the world play its wild song,
With you by my side, I know I belong.
In the symphony of us, we'll forever play,
A melody cherished, day after day.

## Nurtured by Kindness

In gentle gestures, our bond takes root,
Soft spoken words, like whispers of fruit.
With each shared smile, our hearts expand,
Building a future, hand in hand.

Through storms of life, we stand as one,
Guided by kindness, always on the run.
In every act, we sow and grow,
With tender care, our love will flow.

Each moment shared, a cherished gift,
In the quiet, our spirits lift.
With open hearts, we dare to dream,
In a world of wonder, we gleam.

From seeds of hope, great forests rise,
In every sunrise, love's own prize.
Through darkness, kindness lights the way,
In every heart, we'll find the play.

Nurtured by care, we find our voice,
In every struggle, we make the choice.
Together we flourish, forever entwined,
In love and kindness, our hearts aligned.

## The Echoing Footsteps

In the quiet night, they tread,
Footsteps sound where dreams are led.
Whispers linger on the breeze,
Carrying tales from ancient trees.

Each step taken holds a story,
Echoes fade in silent glory.
Paths of shadows intertwine,
Tracing back to moments divine.

The past in every sound we hear,
Memories close, forever near.
Footprints left on wandering trails,
Tracing heartbeats, love prevails.

Through the forest, down the lane,
Every step a sweet refrain.
In the dusk, their shadows blend,
Where the journey finds its end.

In the night, we find our way,
Led by echoes, come what may.
Hand in hand, no fears to mold,
Together, brave and ever bold.

## **Notes of Affection**

In a world of scattered notes,
Whispers carried on soft boats.
Each word penned with tender grace,
Finding shelter in our space.

Melodies of hearts that sing,
Gentle tunes that love can bring.
Like a breeze, they softly sway,
Filling up our every day.

With each touch, our spirits glow,
Notes that dance, a boundless flow.
In the silence, feelings bloom,
Filling every empty room.

Lines of laughter, tears that blend,
Across the pages, hearts transcend.
Written deep in ink divine,
Affection's song, forever thine.

So we share these notes with zeal,
Crafting chords that always heal.
In this symphony we've sewn,
Love's sweet echo found at home.

## Hearts Interwoven

Threads of gold and silver shine,
In each heart, a grand design.
Tangled lives, yet beautifully,
Together spinning destinies.

Fingers clasped in gentle trust,
In the weave, we find what's just.
Every stitch a vow we make,
A tapestry, our love's awake.

In the shadows, colors blend,
Painted visions, hearts suspend.
Patterns rich, with stories told,
In the fabric, brave and bold.

Through the seasons, we align,
Hearts interwoven, so divine.
With each heartbeat, pulse our song,
In this union, we belong.

As we stand, side by side,
In this journey, love our guide.
Together, we will always strive,
In this dance, we come alive.

## The Heartfelt Journey

On a road where dreams unfold,
Stories whispered, secrets told.
Every mile a chance to grow,
In our hearts, a steady glow.

With each sunrise, hope ignites,
Painting skies with warm delights.
Hand in hand through changing light,
Chasing shadows, spirits bright.

Through the valleys, over hills,
Love's embrace, a warmth it fills.
Wanderlust and gentle grace,
In this journey, find our place.

Every turn reveals a view,
Moments shared, forever true.
In the laughter and the tears,
Heartfelt tales that conquer fears.

And as the stars begin to shine,
In our hearts, the paths entwine.
With every step, we start anew,
In this journey, just us two.

## **Merging Streams**

Two rivers flow, side by side,
In whispered dreams where currents glide.
They dance together, smooth and free,
The world around a symphony.

Beneath the trees, the shadows play,
As golden sun greets the day.
With every curve, each bend they take,
New paths of joy they softly make.

The laughter echoes, nature's song,
In every heart, where they belong.
United in their gentle race,
They forge ahead, a warm embrace.

Through stones and banks, they weave their tale,
In unity, they will not fail.
As one they rise, as one they fall,
A bond unbroken, deep and tall.

Together, streams that never part,
Flowing onward, heart to heart.
In the end, we find our dreams,
In love, like life's merging streams.

## **Linked by Light**

Stars above in velvet skies,
Whisper tales, the night replies.
A guiding light, a hopeful spark,
Ignites the dreams that drift in dark.

The moonlit path, a silver thread,
Connecting hearts where shadows tread.
In every shimmer, every glow,
We find the warmth we long to know.

Time flows gently, moments caught,
In every glance, the love we've sought.
Through whispers soft, and gentle sighs,
The truth of bonds that never die.

Hand in hand beneath the stars,
We journey far, no matter the scars.
In every twinkle, bright and bold,
Lie stories of the hearts we hold.

Linked by light, eternally,
In every breath, the harmony.
Together, always, side by side,
In this bright world, our hearts abide.

## In Harmony's Embrace

In forests deep where shadows play,
Nature sings the dawn of day.
Each leaf, a note, each breeze, a song,
In harmony, we all belong.

The river hums a soft refrain,
As sunlight sparkles on the grain.
In every pulse, a heartbeat's trace,
We find our peace in nature's grace.

Beneath the skies, in colors bright,
We gather strength from shared delight.
In laughter shared, in silence, too,
We weave a bond, forever true.

With every step, in rhythm's flow,
Together through the highs and lows.
In unity, our spirits soar,
Embraced by nature, evermore.

In harmony's embrace, we stand,
With open hearts, hand in hand.
A tapestry of love we trace,
In every moment, time and space.

## Harvest of Memories

Fields of gold, where time stands still,
A bounty rich, the heart does fill.
In every grain, a story told,
A harvest shared, a love so bold.

The laughter echoes in the breeze,
As memories gather under trees.
In every glance, a bond we see,
A tapestry of you and me.

With every sunset's golden hue,
We gather moments, proud and true.
In twilight's glow, our spirits dance,
In cherished nights, we find our chance.

Through seasons change, as time rolls on,
The seeds we plant have never gone.
In tender hearts, the past will thrive,
Forevermore, we feel alive.

From every tear and every smile,
We weave a life worth every while.
In harvests rich, forever blessed,
In memories shared, we find our rest.

## **A Garden of Shared Dreams**

In a garden where dreams bloom bright,
We nurture hopes with morning light.
Each petal whispers of tales untold,
Together we flourish, brave and bold.

With every seed that we choose to sow,
Trust and laughter help them grow.
A tapestry of colors intertwined,
In this haven, our hearts aligned.

Under the sun's warm, golden rays,
We share our visions, our endless ways.
The fragrance of joy and sweet delight,
In this sacred space, everything feels right.

As seasons change, we stand as one,
Through storms and shadows, we won't run.
With roots so deep, our spirits soar,
In this garden, we both explore.

Here blooms a love that knows no end,
In each other, we find a friend.
With every blossom, a promise made,
In this garden, our dreams will never fade.

## **Hand in Hand Through Time**

With fingers laced, we walk this road,
Along the path, our stories flowed.
Through laughter shared and silent tears,
Together we combat our fears.

Each moment cherished, time stands still,
With every heartbeat, we climb the hill.
Through shadows cast and sunlight's grace,
We find our way, heart to heart, face to face.

The clock may tick, but we defy,
In love's embrace, we learn to fly.
Hand in hand, we face the dawn,
In this journey, we are reborn.

Each chapter tells of where we've been,
Through twists and turns, thick and thin.
Together we write our own sweet rhyme,
Two souls entwined, hand in hand through time.

In every challenge, we stand as one,
Our love a beacon, a shining sun.
Through life's seasons, vast and wide,
With you, my love, I take great pride.

# Radiant Paths of Companionship

On radiant paths where friendship glows,
We walk together, where kindness flows.
With every step, our laughter sings,
In the journey, joy this bond brings.

Hand in hand through fields of gold,
Every story cherished, every moment bold.
With hearts aligned and spirits bright,
We chase the stars, embracing the night.

Through valleys deep and mountains high,
In each other's light, we learn to fly.
The world around us fades away,
In our companionship, forever we stay.

With every challenge, we rise anew,
In this dance of life, just me and you.
Radiant paths we gladly tread,
With love and laughter as our thread.

In this journey, we find our way,
Through every night and every day.
Two hearts that pulse in unity,
Together, we cherish our community.

## Starlit Conversations

Beneath the stars, we share our dreams,
As moonlight pours through silver beams.
With whispers soft, our secrets flow,
In the night's embrace, our spirits glow.

Each moment shared, a treasure found,
In the quiet night, our hearts resound.
The cosmic dance, a symphony sweet,
With every word, our souls meet.

In starlit skies, we gaze in awe,
Finding beauty in the world's law.
With each heartbeat, our tales unfold,
In this celestial bond, pure and bold.

Through gentle winds and silent sighs,
We weave our dreams beneath the skies.
In laughter, tears, we find our grace,
In starlit conversations, we embrace.

As constellations guide our way,
We share our hopes, come what may.
In each night's hush, we're never alone,
In the universe vast, love has grown.

## The Tapestry of Us

In threads of gold, we weave our days,
Moments stitched in countless ways.
From laughter's light to sorrow's hue,
Together, we emerge anew.

With each knot tied, our bond grows strong,
In rhythm, we find where we belong.
Through shadows cast and sunlit dreams,
We dance in life's intricate seams.

Memories blend like colors bright,
In fabric spun from day to night.
Our tapestry both old and new,
A story told in every hue.

Through trials faced and joys embraced,
Each stitch a moment, perfectly placed.
We craft a tale of love and trust,
A masterpiece, our hearts combust.

So here we stand, in woven grace,
Our tapestry, a sacred space.
Side by side, forever we thread,
In life's grand art, our spirits spread.

## **Unfolding Petals of Joy**

In morning light, the blooms arise,
A dance of colors, vivid skies.
Each petal soft, a gentle sigh,
In nature's hands, we flutter by.

The dew-kissed leaves, they glimmer bright,
As whispers weave through day and night.
With every breeze, a tale unfolds,
Of laughter shared, and love retold.

A garden full, our hearts align,
In fragrant air, sweet moments shine.
Together, we embrace the sun,
Two souls as one, our journey begun.

With every bloom that greets the day,
We find our path along the way.
In vibrant hues, our worries fade,
As joy in life's embrace is made.

So let us dance in fields of grace,
And let our spirits interlace.
For in each petal, love we find,
A garden of the heart and mind.

## Nurtured Souls

In quiet moments, bonds we tend,
With gentle hands, our spirits blend.
Through storms we weather, side by side,
A nourish of love, our hearts abide.

Each word a seed, each hug a beam,
In fields of trust, we dare to dream.
Together, we grow, roots intertwine,
In the garden of hopes, our hearts align.

Through seasons' change, we stand as one,
In laughter's warmth, we find the sun.
With every challenge, mountains we climb,
In the rhythm of life, we dance in time.

A sanctuary we create,
A space of love, no room for hate.
In nurturing ways, we stay awake,
To cherish each moment, to give and take.

So here we are, nurtured and free,
Two souls entwined in harmony.
Through life's sweet journey, hand in hand,
In love's embrace, together we stand.

## The Echoes of Laughter

In the halls of time, laughter rings,
A joyful sound, like flapping wings.
With every chuckle, shadows fade,
A melody of joy, serenely played.

Through moments shared, our spirits soar,
In echoes bright, we seek for more.
With each new dawn, our hearts unite,
In laughter's glow, the world feels right.

From playful jests to tales retold,
In every giggle, our stories unfold.
In friendships deep, we find our place,
In laughter's arms, we embrace grace.

An orchestra of joy, we create,
With every burst, a chance to celebrate.
Through ups and downs, we rise together,
In the symphony of life, love's tether.

So let us laugh, for moments shine,
In the echoes of joy, we intertwine.
For in every smile, life's beauty glows,
A tapestry of laughter, forever flows.

**Treasures of Togetherness**

In the quiet moments shared,
Laughter rings like golden chimes.
Hearts entwined, a bond declared,
Building dreams across the times.

With every smile, a light is born,
Through trials faced, we stand as one.
In every storm, no heart forlorn,
Together, we have just begun.

Echoes of love in whispered sounds,
Hands that hold in gentle grace.
In every heartbeat, hope abounds,
In every prayer, a warm embrace.

In the tapestry we weave,
Colors bright in harmony.
In trusting eyes, we dare believe,
Forever linked, eternally.

For in this treasure, we dwell so near,
The bonds of love will always bind.
Through every joy, through every tear,
Together, peace is what we find.

## **Seeds of Joy**

In gardens where the wildflowers grow,
Seeds of laughter find their place.
Each moment shared begins to flow,
A dance of hearts, a sweet embrace.

Beneath the sun, our spirits soar,
We water dreams with tender care.
In every smile, we find much more,
Together, we rise, so light, so fair.

As autumn leaves begin to fall,
We gather hope in every hue.
In every whisper, hear the call,
The seeds of joy we plant anew.

Each friendship blooms, a cherished thread,
Woven deeply through the years.
In every path that we have led,
We find the strength to face our fears.

So let us nurture, let us grow,
In fields of laughter, side by side.
These seeds of joy, together sow,
In every heart, forever tied.

## **The Unity of Souls**

In the silence where spirits meet,
Two hearts whisper in the night.
A melody soft, gentle, sweet,
In harmony, a timeless flight.

Through the shadows, we find our way,
Each step echoing a common dream.
In tangled paths where spirits sway,
Together, we forge a perfect team.

A canvas painted with every scar,
Each brushstroke tells a tale of grace.
We shine brighter, no matter how far,
In the tapestry of time and space.

With every laugh, with every tear,
We weave a bond that will not break.
In moments shared, we conquer fear,
Hand in hand, with every step we take.

For in this union, we find ourselves,
A legacy of love and light.
In the unity of souls, it dwells,
A gentle glow that fills the night.

## **Wandering Buds**

In the garden where dreams take flight,
Wandering buds begin to bloom.
With every dawn, a new delight,
Each petal bright, dispelling gloom.

Through winding paths, we roam so free,
Curiosity, our guiding star.
In every glance, a mystery,
Our hearts ignited, shining far.

The summer sun warms every soul,
As whispers dance upon the breeze.
Together, we are whole,
With laughter swaying through the trees.

In twilight's glow, we find our peace,
Collecting memories, sweet and rare.
The joy of wanderlust won't cease,
In every heart, love's promise there.

So let us wander, hand in hand,
In every step, a story spun.
For in this journey, we understand,
Wandering buds unite as one.

## The Light We Share

In the twilight glow we meet,
Whispers gentle, hearts replete.
A flicker sparked, a bond so bright,
Together we chase the fading light.

Through shadows cast, we find our way,
Each step forward, come what may.
In laughter shared and silence deep,
The light we share, a promise we keep.

With every dawn, a chance to grow,
In unity, our spirits flow.
Hand in hand, we journey near,
In every heartbeat, love sincere.

When storms may come and skies are gray,
Our light will guide, won't fade away.
For in the dark, we shine the most,
In the warmth, together we boast.

So here we stand, two souls embraced,
In every moment, love interlaced.
The light we share, forever bright,
Together we'll share the endless night.

## In the Heart's Garden

Within the soil, our dreams take root,
Nurtured gently, we cultivate truth.
Each petal blooms, colors collide,
In the heart's garden, love won't hide.

Silent whispers fill the air,
Each secret shared, a bond laid bare.
With every season, we learn to trust,
In the heart's garden, love is a must.

Amidst the weeds, we find our way,
With patience growing day by day.
In every flower, stories entwine,
In the heart's garden, we both shine.

Together we dance in the morning mist,
Harvesting moments we can't resist.
In every sunset, new dreams start,
In the heart's garden, a sacred part.

So let us tend to this sacred space,
With gentle hands, and a warm embrace.
In the heart's garden, we'll forever stay,
Growing together, come what may.

## **The Bridge We Build**

Across the waters, we lay a bridge,
A connection formed, our hearts the ridge.
With every nail, trust is entwined,
In the bridge we build, our souls aligned.

Each step we take, a promise made,
Through storms we'll stand, unafraid.
With laughter and tears, we strengthen the ties,
In the bridge we build, hope never dies.

The winds may howl, the currents strong,
But together we find where we belong.
With every heartbeat, we lay each stone,
In the bridge we build, we're never alone.

So hand in hand, we journey forth,
Embracing dreams of endless worth.
Through valleys deep and mountains high,
In the bridge we build, we learn to fly.

And as the sunset paints the sky,
We'll cross together, you and I.
In love's embrace, we make our stand,
In the bridge we build, forever hand in hand.

## Views from the Same Hill

On the hilltop, we stand so tall,
With open hearts, we embrace it all.
The world below, a tapestry bright,
From views so vast, we find our light.

In every dawn, a canvas anew,
Colors blend in the morning dew.
With laughter shared, our spirits soar,
From views of love, we long for more.

Seasons shift, and time does flow,
Yet here together, we choose to grow.
With every sunset, moments we save,
From views on the hill, our hearts be brave.

As the stars emerge, a guiding spark,
In the night's embrace, we leave our mark.
With shared dreams, our visions connect,
From views on the hill, we'll protect.

So let us marvel at all we see,
Hand in hand, just you and me.
From our perch above, the world feels right,
In the views from the same hill, we ignite.

## In the Shade of Each Other

Under sprawling trees we find,
A refuge from the blazing sun.
Together, hearts and hands entwined,
In silence, love speaks softly, won.

Through whispered winds and rustling leaves,
We shelter dreams, let burdens fade.
In laughter's warmth, the heart believes,
Our world in harmony is made.

With every glance, a story told,
In shadows deep, our bond grows strong.
Within this space, we break the mold,
Together, we always belong.

The daylight fades, the stars ignite,
In twilight's glow, we hold our breath.
For in the shade, love feels so right,
A promise blooms beyond mere death.

So let us cherish this lost art,
Of simply being side by side.
In the shade of each other's heart,
We find the strength, the hope, the pride.

## **Harmonies of Compassion**

In a world that often strays,
Compassion calls, a gentle song.
Together we can find our ways,
In harmonies, we all belong.

With open arms, we share the load,
Each tear a bridge, each smile a ray.
In unity, on love's pure road,
We pave the path, we light the way.

Every act holds strength untold,
A simple touch can heal the heart.
In stories shared, both brave and bold,
We plant the seeds, we play our part.

When shadows fall and spirits wane,
A kind word echoes through the night.
In every struggle, in each pain,
Together we can find the light.

So let our voices rise and blend,
In joyous notes of empathy.
For with each chord, we start to mend,
Creating worlds of harmony.

**Paving the Way**

With every step, we carve our path,
Together facing what may come.
In every choice, in joy or wrath,
We build a road, we beat the drum.

Through winding turns and hills so steep,
We hold the future in our hands.
With faith and hope, we dare to leap,
And forge a bond that understands.

When storms arise and skies turn gray,
We stand as one, unmovable.
In unity, we pave the way,
Our hearts create the indivisible.

With bricks of laughter, tears of joy,
Each moment shared, we lay a stone.
Together, we will not destroy,
The dreams that guide us towards home.

So let us march, unyielding, proud,
With purpose strong and spirits free.
In every promise, in every vow,
We pave the way for all to see.

## **The Roots We Share**

In a garden rich with dreams,
Our roots entwined beneath the earth.
Connected deep in sacred seams,
We nurture love, we cultivate worth.

Through seasons wild and skies of gray,
We stand together, hand in hand.
In every storm, we find a way,
To thrive and bloom, a heartland grand.

The whispers of the past still hum,
In lessons learned, in laughter shared.
Our journeys blend, and yet we come,
To learn that bonds are seldom barred.

With every leaf that sways above,
Our strength is found in unity.
Together we can rise, we love,
The roots we share set spirit free.

So let us honor what we grow,
With patience rich, with care and grace.
For through our hearts, affection flows,
The roots we share will find their place.

## **Echoes of Support**

In shadows deep, we stand as one,
With whispered hopes, our battles won.
Through trials faced, we lift the weight,
In unity, we shape our fate.

Together we rise, through darkest nights,
With every heartbeat, we share our fights.
A chorus strong, we build the walls,
To catch each other when one falls.

A hand to hold, in stormy weather,
We forge a bond that lasts forever.
No voice unheard, no heart left bare,
In every moment, we show we care.

Through laughter shared, we mend our seams,
In echoes bright, we share our dreams.
For every tear, a joy will sprout,
In echoes of support, we weave about.

In circles wide, our spirits dance,
With love and hope, we take the chance.
For every challenge, we find a way,
In echoes strong, we'll never sway.

## A Tapestry of Care

In threads of love, we intertwine,
Each color bright, a story divine.
With tender hands, we weave the light,
A tapestry of care, so bright.

Through ups and downs, we stitch our dreams,
In whispered moments, or so it seems.
The fabric grows, rich with our tales,
In every fold, the heart prevails.

Shared laughter and tears, the fabric sways,
In the warmth of friendship, the spirit plays.
With gentle hearts, we craft and mold,
A tapestry of care, pure gold.

In sunset hues, we find our peace,
With every knot, our love's increase.
The seams may fray, but bonds hold tight,
In a tapestry of care, we write.

As seasons change, the colors flow,
In life's great dance, our spirits glow.
Together we're strong, we face the dare,
In life's embrace, a tapestry of care.

## **Blossoms of Belonging**

In gardens green, our roots entwine,
Where seeds of trust, through time, align.
With gentle hands, we nurture growth,
In blossoms sweet, we find our oath.

Through storms we weather, side by side,
In fields of hope, love's light won't hide.
With petals soft, our hearts expand,
In blooms of joy, we take our stand.

From different paths, we gather near,
In fragrant air, we shed our fear.
Each blossom bright, a story shared,
In a tapestry of love, prepared.

With each small sprout, a bond will form,
Through every trial, we weather the storm.
In the wild embrace, we come alive,
In blossoms of belonging, we thrive.

The seasons change, but roots grow deep,
In fields of belonging, we sow what we reap.
Together we flourish, let the world see,
In blossoms of belonging, we are free.

## Beyond the Horizon

The sun dips low, painting skies wide,
A whispered promise, the stars will guide.
In dreams that stretch, like endless space,
We seek the truth, in every place.

With every step, the path unfolds,
Adventures called, with stories untold.
Through valleys deep and mountains high,
Beyond the horizon, our spirits fly.

In every heartbeat, a chance to be,
With courage bright, we sail the sea.
Through endless night, we find the dawn,
With hope in hand, we carry on.

The journey long, but love will steer,
Through whispered winds, our vision clear.
Together we chase what lies ahead,
Beyond the horizon, where dreams are fed.

For every sunset, a sunrise waits,
In every moment, we shape our fates.
With open hearts, we choose to roam,
Beyond the horizon, we find our home.

## Sheltered Under One Canopy

Beneath the tall branches, we stand true,
Whispers of the leaves call out to me and you.
Together we find comfort, warmth, and grace,
In nature's embrace, we all find our place.

Each shadow holds stories, of laughter and tears,
In the stillness, we banish our fears.
A canopy woven with hope and with trust,
In shared moments, we learn that we must.

United in spirit, under skies so wide,
Our hearts intertwined, with nothing to hide.
Strengthened by roots that grow deep in the ground,
Here, love knows no limits, together we're found.

When storms are a-brewing, we lean on the strong,
Together in shelter, we hum our own song.
No winds can divide what has grown in this space,
With each gentle sigh, we share our embrace.

With sunlight breaking, a new dawn appears,
In the glow of our trust, we conquer our fears.
Beneath this grand canopy, we claim our own way,
Together we flourish, come what may.

## **Trails of Mutual Support**

Along winding pathways, our journeys align,
Side by side walking, hearts that combine.
Each step that we take brings us closer in sync,
Through valleys and hills, together we think.

The weight that we carry, it lightens with time,
In shared strength, we climb, in rhythm, we rhyme.
Fellow travelers, with courage in guise,
We rise in the dawn, with hope in our eyes.

The hills may get steep, but our spirits will soar,
With hands clasped tight, we can weather the roar.
In laughter and kindness, we build what we need,
Our hearts intertwined, we plant every seed.

With each winding bend, new horizons we meet,
Our dreams intertwine, our tapestry sweet.
In moments of silence, our souls intertwine,
On trails of support, our lives brightly shine.

Through rivers we navigate, with trust as our guide,
With courage beside us, we'll boldly collide.
Past mountains of doubt, we'll soar ever high,
On trails of support, you and I will fly.

## Cradled by Kindness

In gentle reflections, we find our embrace,
Cradled by kindness, in this sacred space.
With whispers of comfort, we nurture the heart,
Through gestures of love, we each play our part.

A smile can ignite the flicker of light,
In shadows of doubt, we will shine ever bright.
In moments of kindness, our spirits unite,
We craft a warm world, igniting our flight.

In the stillness of night, kindness becomes,
A guiding star shining, as peace gently hums.
With hands soft and open, we gather the grace,
In circles of trust, our true selves we face.

Through waves of compassion, we flow ever free,
In the sea of our kindness, we nurture the sea.
Each ripple a promise, each act a small grace,
Cradled by kindness, we find our own place.

With hearts ever tender, we welcome the day,
In the glow of our kindness, we'll find our way.
Through the trials of life, let our spirits revive,
Cradled in kindness, together we thrive.

## **Connections in the Twilight**

As daylight begins to softly recede,
We find in the twilight, a moment to heed.
In shadows that lengthen, we gather as one,
With hearts intertwined, until day is done.

The sky painted whispers, of orange and gray,
In this magical hour, we cherish the day.
With laughter like fireflies, dancing around,
Connections in twilight, in silence profound.

Each glance is a promise, each word a sweet thread,
In the tapestry woven, no worries nor dread.
In the twilight's embrace, our spirits align,
As we walk hand in hand, your heart next to mine.

The stars start to twinkle, a gentle display,
In the moments we share, our worries decay.
With dreams generously planted, we start to believe,
Connections in twilight, a gift to receive.

As the night gently wraps us in its lore,
We find in the darkness, our spirits will soar.
Together we're stronger, like constellations bright,
In the magic of twilight, we embrace the night.

## Cherished Moments

In the twilight glow, we sit and dream,
The laughter echoes, soft as a stream.
Each glance we share, a treasure held tight,
In the warmth of our hearts, pure delight.

Whispers of joy dance on the breeze,
Time stands still, bending with ease.
In fleeting seconds, love finds its way,
As cherished moments gently sway.

The world fades away, it's just us two,
Painting our skies in vibrant hue.
Here, in this space, we are alive,
A haven of peace where dreams thrive.

Songs of our childhood play in the air,
As we gather close, banishing care.
Every heartbeat sings of the past,
In these cherished moments, love will last.

So let the hours slip by like sand,
For in our embrace, forever we stand.
Each moment locked in time's gentle clasp,
In life's tender dance, love's sweetest gasp.

## Endless Memories

A photograph fades, but feelings remain,
In the book of our hearts, joy and pain.
Footprints in the sand, washed by the tide,
Endless memories, forever our guide.

As seasons shift, the years roll on,
In whispered dreams, our spirits are drawn.
With every sunrise, new tales begin,
Woven together, where love has been.

Through laughter and tears, we journey afar,
Carrying the light of each shining star.
In echoes of time, we find our grace,
Endless memories, our sacred space.

The canvas of life painted bright and bold,
Every moment tells stories untold.
In the warmth of embrace, we find our peace,
Endless memories, may they never cease.

So let's gather close under the starlit sky,
With hearts intertwined, together we'll fly.
For in every heartbeat, our essence flows,
Endless memories where true love grows.

## The Canvas of Trust

On a canvas vast, painted with care,
Trust is the color that lingers in air.
Each stroke a promise, vibrant and bright,
In shadows and light, we find our sight.

With open hearts, we lay down our fears,
Building a bridge through laughter and tears.
In connection's embrace, our spirits align,
The canvas of trust, a design divine.

Colors intertwine like our hands in play,
In the warmth of connection, we find our way.
Each moment a brushstroke, bold and sincere,
Crafting a masterpiece, year after year.

In shades of remember, we find our place,
A tapestry woven with love's gentle grace.
Through storms we weather, together we'll thrive,
The canvas of trust keeps our dreams alive.

So let us create, each day anew,
With every sunrise, painting our view.
In the artistry of life, hand in hand,
The canvas of trust, forever we'll stand.

## **Echoes of Togetherness**

In the quiet stillness, our hearts beat as one,
As shadows stretch long, merging into the sun.
With whispers of love, our spirits entwined,
Echoes of togetherness, forever aligned.

Through paths we wander, side by side,
In laughter and tears, we take in the ride.
With stories unfolding, rich as can be,
In echoes of togetherness, we find harmony.

The world may be chaos, but here it's us,
In the gentle embrace, we place our trust.
With every soft word, a promise we seal,
Echoes of togetherness, intimately real.

With fingers entwined, we forge our own fate,
Through storms and through sunlight, we patiently wait.
In the depth of our bond, love's symphony plays,
Echoes of togetherness, lighting our days.

So gather me close, let the world drift away,
In this sacred space, together we'll stay.
In echoes of laughter, our hearts will resound,
In the embrace of togetherness, true love is found.

## **Cherishing Each Step**

With every footfall on this winding road,
We gather memories, lightening our load.
Each step a journey, hand in hand we go,
Cherishing each step, through high and low.

In sunny meadows or under grey skies,
With laughter and love, our spirits will rise.
Through valleys of shadow, together we tread,
Cherishing each step, where courage is fed.

The rhythm of life beats steady and true,
In the dance of the moment, it's me and you.
Celebrating each triumph, healing each scar,
Cherishing each step, our guiding star.

As the seasons change and the years swiftly fly,
With hearts intertwined, we reach for the sky.
With gratitude, we treasure the journey we're on,
Cherishing each step, from dusk until dawn.

So take my hand, as the stars start to gleam,
In this voyage of life, together we dream.
Each step is a blessing, let love lead the way,
Cherishing each step, come what may.

## Mutual Raindrops

Gentle droplets dance and play,
Filling up the quiet day.
Nature's rhythm, soft and light,
Bringing life in pure delight.

Each drop whispers secrets vast,
Of the future and the past.
Together they create a song,
In the world where we belong.

Clouds embrace in cool array,
Sharing stories, come what may.
Unity in falling grace,
Nature's love in each embrace.

Puddles form and laughter springs,
Reflecting joy that freedom brings.
In the stillness, hearts will bloom,
Underneath the greyish gloom.

With every drop, we draw near,
In our hearts, we shed no fear.
Together, we shall rise anew,
In the rain, our friendship grew.

## A Canvas of Colors

Brushes dance on page so wide,
Colors mixing side by side.
Strokes of joy, emotions flow,
A vibrant world begins to grow.

Each hue tells a tale so bright,
Capturing dreams in morning light.
Crimson flames and ocean blue,
In this canvas, life feels true.

Shades of laughter, whispers soft,
A symphony where spirits loft.
On this canvas, hearts collide,
With every stroke, our souls are tied.

Golden sunsets rise and wane,
Peaceful moments born of pain.
Art unveils what words can't say,
In this world, we find our way.

Colors blend, and borders fade,
In our hearts, love is displayed.
Together, we create the scene,
In our tapestry, we're seen.

## **Boughs of Understanding**

Beneath the boughs, we sit and talk,
Sharing dreams on this quiet walk.
Leaves whisper tales of those before,
In the shade, our spirits soar.

Branches stretch in unity,
Holding space for you and me.
Glimmers of light through the green,
In this moment, calm and serene.

Roots entwined beneath the ground,
In nature's bond, our peace is found.
The world above fades to a hum,
In this sanctuary, we become.

Time stands still, just us two,
In silence, we find what is true.
With every sigh, the leaves respond,
In this grove, we feel so fond.

Boughs of wisdom, strong and wise,
Reflecting stories from the skies.
Together, we stand hand in hand,
In understanding, we'll forever stand.

## The Whispering Wind

Softly sighing through the trees,
Carrying secrets on the breeze.
It dances light on gentle waves,
Guiding us through life's unknown caves.

Whispers woven in the night,
A soothing touch, so pure, so right.
Every sound, a story told,
Of adventures brave and bold.

Caressing cheeks with tendrils fine,
The wind's embrace, a love divine.
It carries hopes, dreams that we share,
In its song, we find our prayer.

Through valleys deep and mountains high,
It calls to us, we can't deny.
In every gust, a chance to soar,
Together, we can seek for more.

The day may wane, the night may fall,
But in the wind, we hear the call.
Together we'll face what life intends,
Guided always by the winds.

# A Kaleidoscope of Friendship

In every hue a story lies,
Together we paint the skies.
With laughter and whispers shared,
In this bond, we are declared.

Like shifting shades of light,
Our hearts dance in delight.
Through trials, we find our way,
In friendship's warm array.

Each moment a vibrant thread,
In the tapestry we spread.
Colors blend, never fade,
In this love, we're unafraid.

When shadows fall and roam,
We make the world feel like home.
In the chaos, we remain,
Together, we've much to gain.

A kaleidoscope we weave,
In every laugh, we believe.
A journey we choose to share,
In this dance, we are rare.

## Kindred Winds

In whispered breezes we find grace,
Like leaves that flutter, we embrace.
Together we rise and soar,
With hearts that yearn for more.

Through valleys low and mountains high,
Our spirits twine, they never die.
Kindred winds can't be confined,
In knowing hearts, we're intertwined.

With every gust, our dreams take flight,
Painting the canvas of the night.
In shadows deep, we find the sun,
With friendship's warmth, we are as one.

From stormy seas to quiet shores,
We journey forth, forever more.
With laughter echoing in the air,
In every moment, love we share.

Together, through the swirling gales,
We chart our course, and never fail.
In kindness' breath, we find our way,
In kindred winds, we shall stay.

## United in Color

We are the strokes upon the page,
In vibrant tones, we share our stage.
With every touch, a story spun,
United in color, we've just begun.

From deepest blue to fiery red,
In harmony, our hearts are fed.
Each shade a tale of things we've done,
In unity, we overcome.

Through sepia and hues so bright,
We blend together, pure delight.
Our canvas vast, our spirits wide,
In this spectrum, we take pride.

In every corner where shadows may lay,
We bring the light, we chase away.
Together we paint, hand in hand,
In colors bold, we make our stand.

With strokes of love and joy we create,
A masterpiece that won't abate.
United in color, side by side,
Our bond is strong, our hearts are tied.

## **Melodies of Connection**

In every note a feeling flows,
A melody only friendship knows.
In harmonies, our spirits unite,
Creating magic in the night.

Like gentle chords, we weave and blend,
In music, we find our friend.
Through rhythms sweet, our hearts align,
Together, our voices shine.

In laughter's song and sorrow's tune,
We find the strength to commune.
With every strum, the world fades away,
In this symphony, we shall stay.

As echoes linger in the air,
Our bond grows deeper, ever rare.
In crescendos strong, we rise above,
In the melodies, we find our love.

Through every silence, every sound,
In our music, peace is found.
With every heartbeat, let it flow,
In melodies of connection, we glow.

## Dancing in the Rain

Soft drops fall from above,
Whispers of the sky's love.
With each splash, we rejoice,
Nature sings, we find our voice.

Puddles form, we leap with glee,
In this moment, just you and me.
Our laughter mingles with the storm,
Hearts entwined, the magic's warm.

The world fades, it's just us two,
In every drop, a dance anew.
The ground is wet, but spirits soar,
Together we'll forever explore.

Colors blend, gray skies turn blue,
In the rain, our dreams break through.
Each twirl brings us closer still,
In rhythm with the heart's soft thrill.

So, let the thunder crash and roll,
For in this weather, we find our soul.
Dancing, laughing, hand in hand,
In the rain, life's joy is grand.

## **Echoes of Togetherness**

In quiet corners of our hearts,
There's a bond that never parts.
Whispers soft, a gentle grace,
In every smile, we find our place.

Through trials faced, through laughter shared,
In moments lived, we've both dared.
Across the miles, our spirits sing,
In every memory, love takes wing.

Time may test, but still we stand,
Together woven, hand in hand.
The echoes linger, sweet and bright,
In darkness too, we are the light.

Every story, a thread of gold,
In our hearts, forever hold.
When shadows pass and doubts may rise,
Together, we're the sunrise.

So here's to us, to all we share,
In joys and sorrows, memories rare.
Let echoes ring, our voices blend,
In the dance, we will transcend.

## A Quilt of Moments

Stitched with love, each piece a tear,
In every block, a tale to share.
Woven strong, through highs and lows,
In this quilt, our journey shows.

Colors bright, a vibrant thread,
Through laughter lived and tears we shed.
Gathered close, we find our way,
In every stitch, a memory stays.

Faded patterns speak of time,
In every fold, a little rhyme.
From cherished days to quiet nights,
A crafted warmth, our hearts ignites.

Bathed in soft, comforting light,
Together wrapped, we'll face the night.
Each moment's patch, both small and grand,
A tapestry made by hand.

So hold this quilt, this gift of grace,
In its embrace, we find our space.
For every thread will gently bind,
The love we nurture, the ties that bind.

## **The Symphony of Kindness**

In gentle notes, kindness flows,
Each act a melody that grows.
A tender smile, a helping hand,
Together we create this band.

Harmony in every deed,
In every soul, a sacred creed.
From whispers soft to shouts of cheer,
In this symphony, love draws near.

Each kindness shared, a rhythmic beat,
In every heart, it finds its seat.
Through trials faced, we stand aligned,
In this chorus, our lives combined.

Let gratitude rise like the sun,
In this orchestra, we are one.
With every gesture, big or small,
In kindness' call, we rise for all.

So let the music fill the air,
In every note, remind us to care.
Together we'll compose the song,
In kindness, where we all belong.

## **The Firelight of Unity**

In the glow of the firelight's flame,
We gather here, each heart the same.
With whispers of hope, we share our plight,
Together we stand, united by night.

Through shadows we dance, with laughter so bright,
Binding our dreams, our spirits take flight.
Let the embers remind us of love's embrace,
In this circle of trust, we find our place.

From distant lands, our stories collide,
In the warmth of this bond, we take pride.
Every spark shares a tale, rich and profound,
In togetherness, true beauty is found.

As the night deepens, the stars align,
We share in the silence, our hearts intertwine.
No more alone, in the dark we ignite,
The firelight of unity brings us to light.

## **Weaving Dreams**

In the loom of the night, dreams softly spin,
Threads of our hopes, woven from within.
Each shimmer and glimmer, a tale to be told,
With the colors of passion, and hearts that are bold.

We gather the visions, both big and small,
A tapestry formed, we rise and we fall.
With hands intertwined, we craft our own fate,
In this quilt of desires, let's celebrate.

Through valleys of doubt, our dreams pave the way,
Guiding us forward, come what may.
In the fabric of life, each thread is a trust,
With love and with courage, in dreams we must.

So let us weave on, with laughter and care,
Creating a future, together we share.
In the dance of our lives, let our spirits beam,
For together we flourish, in this weaving dream.

## Under the Same Sky

Beneath this vast dome, we stand side by side,
Different paths taken, but hearts open wide.
In the whispers of winds, our stories entwine,
Under the same sky, our souls truly shine.

The stars share their secrets, of love and of grace,
Illuminating faces, as we all find our place.
Together we wander, through wonders unplanned,
With the universe urging us to take a stand.

Sunrise brings promise, each dawn a new start,
With courage and kindness, let hope be our art.
In moments of sorrow or joy, we will find,
That under the same sky, we're all intertwined.

In the embrace of the night, we dream with delight,
No matter the distance, we'll reach for the light.
For in every heartbeat, across land and sea,
Under the same sky, together we're free.

## Joyful Steps

With each joyful step, we dance through the day,
Embracing the moment, come what may.
In laughter and light, we gather our cheer,
Every path that we take brings those we hold dear.

In the garden of dreams, we plant every seed,
Nurtured with love, they grow from our need.
From whispers of hope to shouts of delight,
Together we laugh, under the moonlight.

Every stumble we make, a lesson to learn,
With every twist and turn, our passions still burn.
Through valleys of shadows, we find our own way,
In the rhythm of life, let our joy lead the play.

With hands reaching high, we'll rise and we'll twirl,
In the embrace of the sun, let our hearts swirl.
So let's take these steps, in sync with our dreams,
For joy is the journey, or so it seems.

## **A Symphony of Kindred Spirits**

In twilight's glow, we share our dreams,
Notes of laughter dance in the streams.
Eyes that sparkle, hearts that sing,
Together we make joy take wing.

With every whisper, our souls align,
Harmony woven, your hand in mine.
In the quiet moments, spirits soar,
A symphony of love, forever more.

Through valleys deep and hills so high,
We chase the stars, you and I.
In perfect rhythm, we find our way,
Kindred spirits, come what may.

With every heartbeat, a gentle tune,
Guided by love, beneath the moon.
A melody that never fades,
Together we dance in life's cascades.

As seasons change and time moves on,
The bond we share, forever strong.
In this grand orchestra, we play our part,
A timeless song, a united heart.

## Bridges Made of Smiles

Across the river, a bridge appears,
Crafted from laughter, built on cheers.
With every smile, the gap grows small,
A connection forged, bridging us all.

Hand in hand, we wander wide,
With joyous hearts, we take the stride.
In every glance, a promise bright,
Bridges made of smiles, pure delight.

Through storms and shadows, we will stand,
Each joyful memory, a gentle hand.
Together we shine, come rain or shine,
Creating pathways, love's design.

With open hearts, we share the load,
Finding beauty on every road.
These bridges hold, through thick and thin,
In every moment, let love begin.

As we traverse this beautiful view,
Every shared smile feels like new.
Through laughter's echo, we'll always find,
Bridges made of smiles, beautifully entwined.

## **Heartstrings in Tandem**

With gentle strums, our heartstrings play,
A melody that guides our way.
In perfect time, our souls entwine,
Creating rhythms, divine design.

In quiet whispers, secrets shared,
A tapestry of love declared.
With every heartbeat, we find our truth,
Heartstrings in tandem, eternal youth.

Through every struggle, hand in hand,
Together we rise, together we stand.
As dreams unfold, we share our song,
In harmony, where we belong.

Each note we play, a story told,
Of love and courage, brave and bold.
Through life's challenges, side by side,
With heartstrings in tandem, love is our guide.

In the dance of life, we'll find our beat,
With every step, our hearts repeat.
Together as one, in joy or strife,
Heartstrings aligned, the music of life.

## Dance of Close Companions

In twilight's glow, we take our stance,
With every heartbeat, we join the dance.
In the rhythm of life, step by step,
Together we twirl, a joyful prep.

With laughter's echo, we glide along,
In every whirling, a lovely song.
Through ups and downs, we spin and sway,
Companions close, come what may.

With every glance, the spark ignites,
In synchronized dreams, we reach new heights.
With trust as our guide, we leap and spin,
In the dance of life, love will always win.

In moonlit nights, we show our grace,
With hearts alight, we find our place.
In every turn, a story shared,
A dance of close companions, love declared.

So let us dance until the dawn,
With joy and laughter, we carry on.
Each step we take, a memory made,
In this sacred dance, we won't be swayed.

Milton Keynes UK
Ingram Content Group UK Ltd.
UKHW021127021124
450571UK00005B/66